Plight to Light

poetry in the journey of life

PRIYANKA JAIN

Made with ♥ on the Notion Press Platform
www.notionpress.com

Contents

Contents

THE PLIGHT: The Dark and the Dust.

"Poetry on the times when life is odd, you are lost and yet you are on your own in the journey".

THE DARK

Agony

After Battling all day long,
My thoughts also exhaust,
By the end of the day.
But not my Agony.

After scribbling what tears me apart.
Tons of emotions, fear, guilt.
The ink of my pen falls short.
Not my words.
But nothing calms me until
I sob.

After the party has ended.
I have busted my stress,
Not the loneliness.
It walks with me back,
On my way to home.

After all day you have seen me,
Behaving normal, asual.
Hiding my scars, my invisible wounds.
My soul is left trembled as soon as
the night arrives.
And all I feel again is Just numbness.
Numbness all over.
The agony begins soon.

Awake or Slept

Awake or slept I don't know,
Looking at the rains thinking nothing,
Yet standing sore.

Awake or slept I don't know,
Am I feeling the wind,
Facing the sunshine,
Or just walking the road.

Awake or slept I don't know,
Am I chasing dreams,
Running in the league,
Or just blaming the things.

Awake or slept I don't know,
Am I better than yesterday,
Or just baffled more today.

Awake or Slept I don't know,
What is with me,
Am only craving to know.
Am only craving to know.

Captivated: the feeling of not having a clarity makes one
question their soul their
identity.
Speaking is vulnerable but scribbling is not. I have tried to
scribble what I could not
speak.

Captivated

Captivated by one of the worst feelings,

That is being unsure about my own feelings.

As days pass by I feel like,

Am just drowning and drowning in this,

Sea of frustration more and more.

Having no clue about what I want where I am going.

It's just like am flowing and flowing in this,

Passage of time leaving it unutilized.

Captivated by one of the worst feelings,

That is being unsure about my own feelings.

I feel like am paying the price for my,

Past actions, taken decisions.

Addictions that led me towards self-destruction.

I feel like am the only villain of my life.

And no is to be blamed rather than myself.

Captivated by one of the worst feelings,

That is being unsure about my own feelings.

Am faulty of not knowing what I want,

I am faulty of not searching a way,

Even though after searching a lot.

Captivated by one of the worst feelings,
That is being unsure about my own feelings.
All I know is am in a dark place now.
Where it feels like am leaving a life,
Where there is no realisation of day and night.

Depression: " Depression is such a thing that it does many things to many people, if
you ask each individual about it, they will have their own different versions of the
same thing but pain and suffering will be constant".

Depression

I don't even know what I have lost,
Is it the path where I have to walk,
Or the confidence to walk on the past.
I don't even know this confused
soul is in search of whom.
A helping hand or a,
Partner to Understand.

I don't even know this guilt is,
For what reason.
Even though I try to overcome my,
Past regrets.
When I choose to Start a new journey
I don't understand why the negative
overtakes the positive.
And destroy my confidence Level.

I want to reach out to someone.
And shout out my fears.
But this fear of trust doesn't,
Let me do that too.
I don't know what I have lost!
But I have surely gained the
Prison of depression!
Prison of depression that doesn't
Give me the permission to,
Come out even on a bail.

Death: "The death is such a tragic thing that it takes days,
months and years and
sometimes,
Even an entire lifetime of someone itself to overcome out
of it."

Death

Person to pictures,

Lost among stars.

Where you went leaving us apart.

You were gone for the world,

But you were taken away from us.

Without you,

It's not the days that hurts.

It's the occasions that haunts.

Dreary looks the walls and the other.

Corners of the house.

Back and forth memories flaunts,

as aching sore.

There is no cure for this

absence anymore.

Wish if your loss was a bad dream but

It isn't it's a tormenting reality.

Person to pictures,

Lost among stars.

Where you went leaving us apart.

Leaving us apart.

Every Year: " Each year is different from another one they

say

what if it isn't. "

Every Year

Another Year is gone all those things,
Which I dreamt of still remains as a dream.
All those places where I wanted to wander,
Still remains in my wish list.

Another year is gone all those people,
Whom I wished for are still no
Where to be seen.
All those things in my to-do list,
Have turned one year older yet again.
And am just keeping a count of it.

Another year is gone thinking next one,
Would be different than the gone.
They say everything change but for me.
It feels like only the calendar changes.
Another year is gone, And I feel,
Same about every such gone year.
Every year just seems like a song to me,
Every year runs in same circle for me.

Another year is gone, And I end up,
Dealing with three same things only.
Overthinking, procrastination, uncertainty,
With every passing year I become a pro at it.

Another year is gone,
Every year just seems like a song to me,
Same meaning, same rhythm.
Every year, another year
I just go by it.

I wish

I wish if I had no regrets,
I wish if I had no reasons,
I wish if I Hadn't procrastinated.
And how I wish If I would never,
Had any of these wishes...

I wish to be free, and I wish to fly,
I wish to sing and dance in joy,
I wish I could finally find me,
I wish I could always be on time,
And how I wish if theses wishes,
Could turn my life.

I wish if I could find the escape.
And not the balance.
I wish if I could get peace to
wishes but it's all chaos.
I wish I wish I wish....
And that's how my life has become.
A never-ending wish-list
A never-ending wish-list.

Fear

A turmoil of life,
That shakes our vibes.
From excuse to habit,
How rapidly it spreads its
arms wide.
Dusk or dawn,
Right or wrong,
It doesn't wait to decide.
It just plays with our heart and mind,
From win to lose,
From hope to despair,
It turns the tables every freaking time.
Fear the uninvited guest of life.
Fear the actual Hellion of life.

Pain: "Pain is that truth which is just hidden behind many masks"

Pain

I have a pain which lives with me,
A pain unwelcomed yet which stays with me.
It wakes up with me, it sleeps with me.
It laughs with me; it hides with me.
Together we are inseparable.
But this pain just doesn't
make me weak.
It also does makes me strong.
I have a pain which lives with me,
A pain unwelcomed yet which stays with me.

This pain When it forms,
The shape of tears.
I don't like it my body doesn't like it.
But somewhere my soul is at peace.
This pain which came in my life.
First hurted me, later changed me.
This pain first mocks me.
And then preaches me.
I have a pain which lives with me,
A pain unwelcomed yet which stays with me.

Pain is like that frenemy who is neither,
My friend nor enemy.
Pain is just pain who keeps appearing,
Like semester exams often and often.
And vanishing like vacations once in a time.
It's a messy relationship after all.
But just as every other relationship
my relationship with pain will also,
not find its perfect ending.
Infact it will try to find a perfect balance.
I have a pain which lives with me,
A pain unwelcomed yet which stays with me.

Suffering

There is suffocation inside the chest,
Which is burning daily like a fire.
How will my soul remain calm?
When there is a guilt lying there.
How do I do repentance of this guilt
So that the devil inside me stop
Playing with my emotions.

There is a misery inside the soul.
Which is growing as large as a tree.
How will my soul remain calm?
When this past keeps re-attacking me.
How do I tackle with this past.
So that the devil inside me stop
playing with my emotions.

There is a void in my life.
Which is filled by people.
How shall I let in someone else in my life?
When trust was played every single time.
How do I trust again?
So that this fear vanishes from life.
So that the devil inside me stop
playing with my emotions.

Trapped: "A state of mind where it's only you vs you."

Trapped

My soul is trapped hoping for a release,
My soul is lost even without an actual defeat.
My soul cries in silence.
My soul is burning alive.

My soul is drowning in overthinking,
My soul is facing an identity crisis,
Every time when I say I am fine,
My soul is left dejected over a hundred times.

Yet I am scared to open up
about it on the outside.
Which kills me daily on the inside.
Because it's not about the sober state.
It's about the judgement people make.

My soul is trapped hoping for a release,
My soul is lost even without an actual defeat.
My soul wanders on the streets
On days and nights,
Searching for a safer space.
Where it can set all its Miseries free
All its Miseries free.

THE DUST

"After the dark we have reached the dust, the dark is about ourselves but the dust

is

About our surroundings"

Corporate Gimmicks: "You can't talk much you can't trust
much you are only
supposed to understand here".

Corporate Gimmicks

So many people, So many faces.
All have here hideous intentions.
Some act sweet when in need.
And rest of the times
all remain hoggish.

An Unofficial rat-race runs here every year.
Friends turn foe in a minute here.
Hardworking one's remained foolish.
While others get ahead with petty tactics.

The pressure here once faces is unmeasurable.
How I wonder they promote
"Mental well-being here".
It effects other areas of life indeed.
Well, nobody speaks on it.
But it takes days, months, or years.
To Come out of the stress of
Corporate Gimmicks indeed!!!

Home

After years of being in home,
I am still finding a home.
A home where I could,
Speak to people not just to walls.
A home where my voice wasn't,
Muted at times but was given support.
A home where equality found.
Its proper place.
Instead of lying beneath the egos.
A home where dreams are,
Given wings to fly.
and not to let it die.
A home where happiness was meant,
To be felt and not to be found.
After years of being in a home,
I am still finding a home,
Where I could feel I belong.
And not just tag along.

I am racing against time

I am racing against time in my present,
To secure my future.
That future which I don't even follow by heart.
In my heart I love my passion and slowly it only
grows even further.
Yet am still joining pieces of my passion.
To create an art which will rule on the hearts,
Which will open the doors to my dreams my desires.

I am racing against my time to plan a travel,
A travel which I always plan but not execute.
In my heart I want to be free like a bird and fly.
Yet am still here sitting under the same roof.
A roof where I can be, but not the roof I want to see.

I am racing my time to manage and improve myself.
Yet most of times am just lazy.
In My heart I make a resolution,
Yet it dissolves like faster than sugar in water.
I am racing against my time to be counted amongst it.
But I am only losing years and gaining fomo all time.

I am racing against time for many things.
that I want yet am still crawling on everything
to make it mine.
I am racing against time everytime.
I am racing against time everytime.

Incompleteness

The feeling of being right and wrong,
The feeling of being noticed and unnoticed,
The feeling of trolls and compliments,
I know it all, I know it all.

The feeling of hopelessness,
The feeling of discontent,
The feeling of acceptance and
Abandonment.
I know it all, I know it all.

The feeling of cravings,
The feeling of musings,
The feeling of togetherness to
The feeling of separation
I have seen it all.

All these feelings just,
Support one feeling.
And that feeling is.
Feeling of incompleteness Altogether.
Feeling of incompleteness Altogether.

Introvert: "You know what the word means but do you know why the word or people exist"

Introvert

Don't ask me if am a introvert.
Instead try to understand why am one.
Maybe I never wished to become one.

Don't think am not interested.
I take my sweet little time to open.
Stay and observe or give me a chance.
Rather than just terming me as
Boring enough...

Fun doesn't have a single meaning.
Your fun is just different than ours.
That's where socialising comes.
You prioritise it; we try to understand it.

Don't ask me if am a introvert.
Instead try to understand why am one.
Maybe I never wished to become one.
Maybe I never wished to become one.

Karma: "Sometimes it's difficult to understand the role of Karma in life and it becomes even more difficult to believe when we fail to understand it".

Karma

After learning the fact karma.
I started following honesty.
It made me so naive that,
The world made a mockery of me.

After learning the fact karma.
I started believing in good deeds,
Following good deeds,
It made me a person that,
People started revelling my sanity.

After learning the fact karma.
I saw things happening to me,
as your sign god.
I followed the path and still.
I only ended up being lost.

After learning the fact karma.
I thought it will reward me,
For my work but little
Did I knew it was all karma?
Testing me after all.
With its karma game, karma game.

The First Lie

Sometimes I wonder who said,
The first lie?
And what it might have been?
Till when that lie might have
had its own run.
In that run don't know
What that lie might have broken.
What rifts it may have created?
What hopes it might have ended.
Today the world is weaved,
In a web of lies.
And every time someone lie's
Innocence dies.
Sometimes I wonder who said,
The first lie?
Wish it was never spoken.
Wish innocence and honesty.
Shouldn't have lost.
Shouldn't have lost.

Memories: "Life is made up of memories only make sure that you make mostly good one's".

Memories

Some Memories are bundle of joys,
Some memories are blunders of life.
Some memories are like winters,
Blowing breeze.
Some memories are like summers,
Scorching heat.
Some Memories doesn't let us sleep,
Some awakens us from the sleep.
Some memories arise out of love,
Some memories arise out of
Lack of love.
Some memories are full of
Blissful-beautiful Moments.
Some memories are full of
Painful-tragic events.
Some memories fade away with time,
Some memories remain uneased in life.
Some memories remain uneased in life.

The Trip: "Some journey Some stories are not always remembered for their happy endings, they are remembered for their unpleasant incidents".
For such unforgettable trips

The Trip

Time flew by but memories of that trip,
Still flashes in front of my eyes.
As I go by the moments of the trip,
I feel ecstatic.
All I wish is to dive in that moment,
And re-live all those once again.
But then there is a thud on my thoughts!
As I come near to the end of this trip.
A staggering storm pushes me,
back in reality.
Since the end of the trip was a bitter-sore memory.
Every time I go on a flashback ride onto this trip,
It leaves me with broken pieces.
Still lying there to collect it.
A trip which I took with great enthusiasm.
Now is a trip,
A trip which I remember only to
Forget more, but I Can't forget.
I can't forget, more of it.

"You have successfully crossed the plight stage now it's time to relax and enjoy a bit before we move forward to the light stage".

Because it's Interval Time

Interval

The beginning of the life was raw,
The later part was inevitable.
After all this plight I Come into
This phase of life.
Where time is fast, but things are slow.
Where life needs to be eased down.
It isn't though.
Where most of them are settled yet am unsettled.
With my goals, my dreams, my journey.
Am sailing on along with the flow.
With unsettled things in hand,
Paving all along the way.
I have somehow reached the interval.
Part of my life.
Just like a filmy story am also wanting,
This interval period to end soon.
Hoping for the dark to evade
And looking forward for change
which welcomes ahead.
In this interval period am there where am
Supposed to be.
But once it's over
Soon I will be there where I wish to be.
Where I wish to be.

THE LIGHT

"Amid the dark and the dust always keep hoping and looking for the bright and the better".

"Hope this Light helps you restore your flaws, Hope this Light continue to guide you

And help you cherish life".

Aroused My soul

Everytime I run, I run for you.
Everytime I wish, I wish about you.
Everytime I pray, I pray for you.
If there is anything apart from you,
For me there is nothing.
Because you for me are my forever.
You make me say a thousand words,
You make me do a thousand things,
Your presence is an endless feeling.
You have aroused my soul by your love,
You have aroused my soul by your smile,
With you I feel the beauty of life.
You have aroused my soul.

Your sweet talks uplifts,
My mood swings.
Your gesture's makes my
Heart swing.
You bring me back to life.
When I am with you.
When the day ends,
I miss Being with you.
You have aroused my soul by your love,
You have aroused my soul by your smile,
With you I feel the beauty of life.
You have aroused my soul.

I want to fly high in your love,
I want you to take a deeper dive in
My soul.
I want to travel the world with you,
I want to feel the deep nature along,
With you.
I want to create moments that,
Feel like magic together with you.
Everytime when you look in my eyes.
I want to look more prettier in your eyes.
You have aroused my soul by your love,
You have aroused my soul by your smile,
With you I feel the beauty of life.
You have aroused my soul.

Be You: "Be your own authentic self in this world be you be unique".

Be You

In the days and in the nights,
Against the odds and even's,
In the dark and in the light,
During the battle of life.
Speak with uprightness.
Share with kindness.
Smile with no regrets,
Hope like always,
Chase it like Nevertheless.
Protect your secrets.
Play it with smartness.
Most importantly love yourself.
Be yourself with no filters attached.
Be you, be you someone,
Somewhere might be getting inspired by you.
So believe in yourself always
Be yourself always.

Desire: "Desire is the starting point of anything and everything"

Desire

I don't desire the sky,
All I desire is just to be on the ground,
From where people aim to fly.
And I will make my own sky.

I don't desire the thousands,
I only desire a few who can,
Spread my work among thousands.
And from there I will build my own tribe.

I don't desire big days,
I just desire days where,
Am working to make it big.
And from there everything will,
Fall in place.

I don't desire the miracles,
I just desire the faith.
And I know it has the power,
To turn any tide.

I don't desire the sky,
All I desire is just to be on the ground.
From where people aim to fly,
And I will make my own sky.

May

May you in anyway,

You believe on the brighter side.

Look at the better side.

May all your chances get,

You a yay!

May you let go everything,

That creates fences in your way.

May you keep finding,

one or the other way.

May you in some way,

You let your manifestations,

Uncover in Mystical ways.

May you in anyway,

You believe on the brighter side.

Look at the better side.

May you always be growing.

And glowing each and everyday.

It's time to rise and shine

It's time to rise and shine,
It's time for dreams to meet the life.
Time for the dark night to end its spell,
Time for the sunlight to
bless the new chapter of life.

It's time for no self-doubt now.
Time to leave the past behind and
move ahead with zero regrets.
Dump the junk feelings,
Manifest only good thoughts,
It's time to acknowledge the new.

It's time for today it's time for now.
It's not the time to think,
It's time to take a step ahead,
Start this journey.
And reach the destination.

It's time to rise and shine,
It's time for dreams to meet the life.
Time for the dark night to end its spell,
Time for the sunlight to
bless the new chapter of life.

I Love The Moonlight: "For all the selenophile's out here"

I Love The Moonlight

I love the moonlight.
Amidst the chaos,
I am a secret admirer.
Of true love.
The cool breeze,
Which peace's out my mind.
The smell of wet soil,
After it rains.
The scenic beauty of the skies,
I prefer drooling over it a hundred times.

I love the moonlight.
I find solace in chilling weather,
Which gives positive vibes.
A long drive listening to soothing music,
Is my weekend life.
There is nothing to show or hide.

I love the moonlight.
Early morning chirping
sounds of the Birds.
The waves of the ocean
Resonate my life,
Which are always high and low,
Yet many love the flow.
Similar are my parents.
They love me to the core.

I love the moonlight.
The birds flying high in the air,
Fearless ambitious touching
the skies.
Are my inspiration in life.
I love the moonlight.
Amidst the chaos,
I am a secret admirer of
True love.

Keep Going: "it is easy to quit anything but difficult is to continue and to keep believing And keep on going".

Keep Going

One day I will fly high.
One day the world will cherish,
My chronicle.
One day all my desires will come true.
So no matter what,
I will keep going until,
The chances run out.
I will keep moving,
Until my breath goes on.
I will stand in the queue,
Until my turn comes.
I will face every hurricane,
Making belief my only way.
I Will keep doing what I do.
Because that is only the plan,
Of my life to keep going.
Until I win or survive.

The Journey

The road is a lengthy or smaller one
doesn't matter.
Am walking on the road just that matters.
The road will lead me to my destination,
or will I face a roadblock doesn't matter.
All I know is I choose this road and faith only counts.
In this road I choose the people, not the fear.
I choose the opportunity, not the lack of trust.
I am carrying both versions of the shy and the bold.
But as the journey progress the shy will take a u turn.
And the bold will continue to move on.
I have started this journey with a hope.
And will end it only with a note.
To keep taking such more journeys
On a roll.

Will You: "Will you honestly give a review of the book
Will you like me to write another poetry book"?

Will You

Will you store me in your heart,
Will you let my memories flow in your
Brain.
Will you let me come in your dreams,
Will you let me step in your joys,
Will you let me listen to your sorrows,
Will you let me create some memories
With you.
Will you let me feel special for you?
Will you let me be the only one for you?
Will you let me be the only one
For you?

What does happiness look like?

What does happiness look like?
Does it look like having a social life,
Or it is having a life of your own people.
Is happiness related to freedom?
Which comes with a price.
Or inner peace which is the
Greatest prize.
Is happiness a score card?
Does it has a qualifying Criteria?
Happiness is just a happy feeling.
Stop attaching things to happiness.
Happiness is in everything.
From being in a party to, reading a book.
From being adventures too silently,
Gazing at the moon.
From following your dreams,
To laying in your mom's lap.
From watching a movie,
To eating a cotton candy.
Happiness doesn't need Society's approval.
Happiness is only about your true calling.
So what does happiness look like?

Happiness looks like you, me and
everyone else.
Being happy in our own space.

• 71 •

We began From Plight We end
at the Light.
We Began from Agony we end
at the Happiness.

This is not the end this is just a
formal goodbye.
I will always stay connected
through my words to you.

Thank You :)

www.ingramcontent.com/pod-product-compliance
Lightning Source LLC
Chambersburg PA
CBHW021129130726
47988CB00003B/1224